THE WOLF AT THE END OF THE BLOCK

THE RIGHTLYND SAGA

Rightlynd

Exit Strategy

Sender

Prowess

The Wolf at the End of the Block

Red Rex

Lottery Day

THE WOLF AT THE END OF THE BLOCK

-⚔ A PLAY ⚔-

IKE HOLTER

NORTHWESTERN UNIVERSITY PRESS

EVANSTON, ILLINOIS

Northwestern University Press
www.nupress.northwestern.edu

LIBRARY OF CONGRESS
CATALOGING-IN-PUBLICATION DATA

Names: Holter, Ike, 1985– author. | Holter, Ike, 1985– Rightlynd saga.
Title: The wolf at the end of the block : a play / Ike Holter.
Description: Evanston, Illinois : Northwestern University Press, 2020. | Series: The Rightlynd saga.
Identifiers: LCCN 2019043195 | ISBN 9780810141605 (trade paperback) | ISBN 9780810141612 (ebook)
Subjects: LCSH: Hispanic Americans— Violence against—Illinois—Chicago— Drama. | Police—Illinois—Chicago— Drama. | Chicago (Ill.)—Drama.
Classification: LCC PS3608.O49435985 W65 2020 | DDC 812/.6—dc23
LC record available at https://lccn.loc.gov/ 2019043195

CONTENTS

PRODUCTION HISTORY

The world premiere of *The Wolf at the End of the Block* was produced by Teatro Vista (Ricardo Gutiérrez, Executive Artistic Director) in Chicago on February 4, 2017. It was directed by Ricardo Gutierrez, with scenic design by Milo Bue, costume design by Uriel Gómez, lighting design by Diane D. Fairchild, sound design by Eric Backus, and props design by Jamie Karas. The production stage manager was Stephanie Hurovitz. The cast was as follows:

Abe . . . . Gabriel Ruiz
Miranda . . . . Ayssette Muñóz
Nunley . . . . Bear Bellinger
James. . . . . .James D. Farruggio
Frida . . . . Sandra Márquez

The Wolf at the End of the Block was produced by 16th Street Theater (Ann Filmer, Artistic Director; Maeli Goren, Managing Director) on April 5, 2018. It was directed by Lili-Anne Brown, with scenic design by José Manuel Díaz-Soto, costume design by Rachel Sypniewski, lighting design by Cat Wilson, sound design by Barry Bennett, and props design by Jesse Gaffney. The production stage manager was Casie Morell. The dramaturg was Kendra Miller. The cast was as follows:

Abe . . . . Alberto Mendoza
Miranda . . . . Gabriela Diaz
Nunley . . . . .Tony Santiago
James. . . . . Christian Isely
Frida . . . . Stephanie Diaz

The Wolf at the End of the Block was commissioned by Teatro Vista, Chicago; Ricardo Gutiérrez, Executive Artistic Director.

THE WOLF AT THE END OF THE BLOCK

CHARACTERS

Abe. Early thirties, Latino. Never knows what to do with his body. Honest to a point, cares for his family and friends, quick temper; always on the bottom but won't give up.

Miranda. Latina. Abe's sister. Finally escaping from a messed-up past; over energetic and eager to fight for any cause. Thirsty for the next step. Loves her brother something fierce. Kind and approachable but will lay down the law without question.

Nunley. Black. Owns a deli. Abe's boss. Guy's guy, fast-talking, people person, aggressive and territorial. Big brother to all those without.

James. White. Cop. Nice guy. Plays dumb. Fiercely intelligent. Old school Chicago. Drinks too much beer. Physically imposing but strangely conversational. Wants to do the right thing, even if it's wrong. Never has to shout; there is no question of his authority.

Frida. Latina. Reporter. Free spirit who's a bit broken down by the system. Has to fight for everything, even when the stakes are low. Knows what she wants. Smooth talker until she needs to strike hard and fast. Can read the instructions on the back of a cereal box and make it sound like an exposé.

NOTE: A slash mark (/) in a character's speech means another character has already started their next line; it's an overlap, and both characters are speaking at the same time. An ellipsis (. . .) in lieu of speech indicates that the characters exchange something silent and necessary. Parenthetical speech means it's an aside; not silent, but not drawing too much attention.

SETTING: Early winter in Rightlynd, Chicago. A gas station, an alley, a park bench. The set is minimal, a couple of bar chairs.

GAS STATION

[*No set.* ABE *is bleeding from the head and the nose, clothes torn up. Looks like shit; it's shocking. He holds a phone in his hand, but addresses the audience directly.*]

ABE [*On edge. Trying to fake like he's not. Beyond shock.*]: I mean I've been—
So I know what *it's like to run,*
I mean I've been doing it uh maybe once, twice a week, my whole life, like since since maybe fourth grade, was it, did *what do you call it* what do you call it uh—
did the cross country no, no, there's another name I—
Can't think of it right now but I grew up doing it
it's part of my life, I know how to, how to like move fast, OK, one of my talents kind of like some people—TRACK.
Track team, not cross country, track. Um.
Sometimes when I get to a new place, like if I'm in a weird party or a new block or the train—just in general, you know, "on the train"—
I get in, and I glance around, and the first thing I do after I get in and glance around is look for my way out, my Dad was—*sorry*

I'm Abe, by the way hi, hi, hahaha, my name's Abe, nice to meet you, hi um . . . I don't usually do this.
Run up to gas stations in the middle of the night, panting, I don't usually: this is not like part of my *daily commute*, you know, hahahaha, I don't just, I don't just leave without charging my phone, I'm like a . . . Kinda on edge kinda . . . Thank you for— listening to me thank you for—

[*He touches behind his head. There's blood.*]

It'll go away, nothing big, it's nothing, just a . . .
So I run. I told you that, right, I—
I run for fun now (once, twice a week) don't do it for track any-more (not now) no I run to get some aspect of my life back I run so so so I can have some kind of pressure uh and it's fun and I'm good at it I'm real good at it and as soon as I left there, as soon as I left there I knew I had to run, and that's why—

[*Feels behind his head.*]

See, it stopped. Drying, already dried, already—
. . . Thank you. Didn't have to do it, but it meant a lot, nice of you, here's a—

[*Takes money out from his wallet.*]

I know you're not a doctor, but who doesn't like a tip, right, who doesn't like . . .

[*Offers a handful of cash.*]

Please. If anyone—if anyone ever, ever asks, tell 'em—
Please.
You tell them I was never here.

NUNLEY: Where the hell is that fucker.

[*Instantly, we're in an—*

ALLEY

The next morning. There's steps and a door and an ashtray. NUNLEY *smokes, wearing a cheap suit;* MIRANDA *eats an entire sandwich.*]

MIRANDA: "He's late."

NUNLEY: He's late, he's late again, and I'm telling you / alright—

MIRANDA: Tell me, / talk about it.

NUNLEY: I'm telling you that *this is it*, you know, and people talk, / too . . .

MIRANDA: What do people / talk about?

NUNLEY: People talk and they say "this is the last time" *and this,* / right now—

MIRANDA: This is what that / *is, right?*

NUNLEY: This right now is exactly *what that is*, and this isn't the first / time,

MIRANDA: "Oh no," / watch out now.

NUNLEY: Oh no, see, the first time it's understandable, second time "Sure, sure, alright then," third time / it's a problem—

MIRANDA: One two three strikes you're out.

NUNLEY: But this ain't even the third / time.

MIRANDA: What time is it?

NUNLEY: *This time's the fourth time!*

MIRANDA: OHHHHHH / HHHHHHHHHH SHIT! Oh, shit!

NUNLEY: It is *past due*, already finished, call the umpire, call the coroner, put a sign on the door / he's out.

MIRANDA: That's right that's right that's right. *Fire his ass, wooo!*

NUNLEY: . . . But I don't wanna like *fire him*, / alright I don't wanna do *all that*—

MIRANDA: Mmhmmm.

NUNLEY: Yeah, see, I mean I'm like a nice guy, I'm like an *approachable guy.*

MIRANDA [*mouth full*]: *Youfugpllle.*

NUNLEY: What t—?

MIRANDA: *Youfugpplle,* YOUFUG / PLLE, youfugggggg—

NUNLEY: Sorry but I've no clue to what the fuck you are trying to say to me right now—*enunciate*, woman, *swallow.*

MIRANDA [*swallows*]: You. Hug. People.

NUNLEY: Thank you, *I hug people.* / I'm a hugger, I let people know I appreciate them.

MIRANDA: (ohmygod) "I hug people" / (ohmygod).

NUNLEY: Like when someone has a problem—

MIRANDA: Alejandro's got like three hundred problems / (amiright?)

NUNLEY: *Abe*, come on "Alejandro" / come on with that hahahaha.

MIRANDA: That's his name I'm saying his name there's a long line of Alejandros what the fuck did the Abes of the world ever do?

NUNLEY: FREED THE SLAVES / DAMN, WOMAN!

MIRANDA: OK OK OK facts are just circumstantial ohmygod I'm on your side Nunley / (ohmygod).

NUNLEY: Thank you, now see your brother *has a big problem,* / right?

MIRANDA: Big problem yes / yes yes.

NUNLEY: See he's got a big problem coming in late he's got a big problem showing up sassy, / OK, *he does that—*

MIRANDA: "Oooh he's so sassy, watch / out now."

NUNLEY: Right, big problems, he's got big problems doing his goddamn job—

MIRANDA: And paying rent on time and turning off the stove and putting / the shower curtain closed after a fucking shower and— (woooooow).

NUNLEY: ("that's getting domestic" i don't care) but when someone has a problem, see, I look at the other factors, (shut up) see, I look at their *home life,* I look at their life-life, I look at what I'm not seeing, what they're not showing me, 'cause every single thing that adds up to a lot *always starts at home.*

MIRANDA: "Home life stays at home."

NUNLEY: Wow, that's super dramatic.

MIRANDA: It's really not though.

NUNLEY: Did you just *cheat out?* This is getting / really dramatic.

MIRANDA: Don't fucking come for me, Nunley, don't . . . See, now, Frida says / we—

NUNLEY: No more 'bout Frida / please—

MIRANDA: *Frida is essential.*

NUNLEY: That woman thinks she's Shaun King but she's really just Gayle, nobody gives a shit about Gayle unless she got Oprah, / where's Oprah now?

MIRANDA: OK this is the biggest brown lady blowing up since Oprah, don't / get it twisted, Nunley

NUNLEY: Fine what she say what she say, *sorry*, / what she say?

MIRANDA: Thank you THANK YOU, look, she got me off my ass, OK, if it weren't for her I wouldn't know about anything going on in Chicago, at all, like I wouldn't know about our evil fucking alderman, I wouldn't know about school protection, OK, I wouldn't even have any idea what stores in my neighborhood are owned and operated by people of color.

NUNLEY: The alderman's office is on the corner, there's a knocked-down school down the block, and I'm a man of color, hello, you are literally eating food from my store, open your eyes, girl, / goddamn.

MIRANDA: She is Saving-My-LIFE because she believes that everyone can make a difference; that's why I got that new website.

NUNLEY: Ain't even finished yet.

MIRANDA: That's why I'm in the process of getting my new website.

NUNLEY: It's actually just a Tumblr / so—

MIRANDA: It connects to my Snapchat and my Twitter, it's for the postmillennials *you wouldn't understand,* / anyway, moving on, so—

NUNLEY: Hahahahahahahaha!

MIRANDA: Frida says, "You show up ten minutes before, you're early; you show up five minutes before and you're on / time."

NUNLEY: That's not a thing.

MIRANDA: *Yes. That is a thing* and we stick by it now, he knows that rule, *I told him to live by that rule,* he cannot avoid that rule 'cause you know I got her calendar on the bathroom wall and he sees that shit every morning.

NUNLEY: Since when did news reporters start getting bathroom calendars?

MIRANDA: It's a Dollar Store calendar, you can put it in any room you want.

NUNLEY: And you chose the bathroom.

MIRANDA: Fuck the fuck off, now look, he can see it, he's got it in his head so why can I arrive places ahead of schedule no problem meanwhile his ass walks in late? Why is that why is that why is that why is that, why?

NUNLEY: Maybe 'cause he works two jobs and you don't even work one?

MIRANDA: That is like offensive, actually, that is like an offensive line / of questioning actually.

NUNLEY: How is that offensive, how, Miranda, *where is your job at /tho?*

MIRANDA: I'm busy.

NUNLEY: Doing . . .

MIRANDA: Projects.

NUNLEY: Like what, like checking your messages, "that's a project"; cleaning the ceiling fan, that's a project; emptying out the dishwasher, "ohmygod it's been such a productive timeline."

MIRANDA: Uh we don't even have a ceiling fan so that is inconsequential, basically, back to this OK what / I'm—

NUNLEY: *He* doesn't have a ceiling fan.

MIRANDA: That's what I just said.

NUNLEY: No you said "we" as in both y'all pay rent, you don't, *he does*, see that's a *singular fragment* and you just tried to turn it into a conjoined enterprise / Miranda, come on—

MIRANDA: Cut the shit, this is darkly suspicious.

NUNLEY: How is this shit darkly suspicious?

MIRANDA: He didn't *come home last night*. Alejandro—*Abe*. He didn't come home / last night.

NUNLEY: Well yeah, was probably with, probably with Jania or probably / like—

MIRANDA: Probably "with, like," who, Nunley, probably with who, he doesn't see anybody, who. Nothing's safe out there anymore. You read the news and you heard what happened to Carlos and Rosa, and don't act like you don't know, Nunley, you know, and as nice as it is inside your little store with all the same people and all the same kind of brown, as nice as it always is in here, *it is not safe for us* out there.

MIRANDA AND NUNLEY: . . .

NUNLEY: You got high this morning.

MIRANDA: Not like a lot.

NUNLEY: Uh-huh.

MIRANDA: It was still dark outside and I have slight vertigo and it was just resin, OK, resin doesn't fucking count, *you know I'm right, Nunley* . . . I worry about my brother so much it makes me— When he doesn't pick up his phone and then I look at the TV and I keep thinking "maybe he didn't have an ID, maybe they just thought he was somebody else, maybe that's all they need, maybe maybe maybe maybe / maybe"

NUNLEY: That's a lot of maybes.

MIRANDA: But you wouldn't know, you don't care, / you don't—

NUNLEY: Uh, I / care—

MIRANDA: About the bottom line and who gets in at nine, / that's it.

NUNLEY: That's my best friend.

MIRANDA: That's my brother and that's all I got, I love him more than myself and I'm trying not to cry right now because if anything if if if anything happened to—
Nothing else matters to me but making sure
He
can
breathe.

[ABE *approaches, exhausted.*]

MIRANDA: You stupid dick-licking waste of airspace, / where the fuck were you, dickface? I hate you! / (OhmyGOD. OhmyGOD.)

NUNLEY: Twenty-two minutes, man, / twenty-two minutes—

MIRANDA: He doesn't care, he never / cares, look at he's he's like "Uhhhh." (Just like uhhhhh.)

NUNLEY: That's a new record, man, that's, that's like an entire episode of prime-time network / TV man that's long—

MIRANDA: Are you OK, what's happening, come here come here what's happening, / are you OK—

NUNLEY: Oh so now you're hugging him, now / that's what's up, OK.

MIRANDA. Of course I'm hugging him, / back off.

NUNLEY: Yo, she told me to fire you not five minutes ago, / bro.

MIRANDA: It was a coping mechanism, he coulda been dead THERE WERE A LOT OF MAYBES . . . Ohmygod what happened to / your—

ABE [*flinching from her touch*]: Don't do that—

MIRANDA: What's wrong with your / face, you're bleeding—

ABE: Nothing's wrong with my face, can you go home please?

MIRANDA: Wow, / wow-wow-wow-wow-wow.

ABE: No I'm sorry I'm sorry I'm just just, it's been a night, OK, it's been a—
Just need to run to the bathroom, I'll be fine, I'll be fine, uh, you get a sandwich.

MIRANDA: I don't just come here for the sandwiches, OK.

NUNLEY: (She shoved the whole thing in her mouth like a fucking badger, / so—)

[NUNLEY *exits into the store.*]

MIRANDA: Yes, those are facts, / he is correct, still, hello, look at me, Abe, hello, HEY, right here—

ABE: Where you going?

NUNLEY: Checking the back room, / what's going on, what's happening, we good—

ABE: No, uh fuck uh (ONE SECOND OK). Nunley, leave me the back room, go check the counter, I'll be in in a second, I'll jumpstart the coffee and the juicer / and all that crap, don't worry about it.

NUNLEY [*exiting*]: "Check the counter," telling me what to do, bossing me around with his late ass / and what not . . .

MIRANDA: I'm not leaving, FYI, I'm / not moving.

ABE: Gotta get to work, Miranda, gotta keep moving / if I stop—

MIRANDA: You are bleeding out of your face, you're wearing the same clothes from yesterday, you look like walking shit, what the hell are those *Lord of the Ring* things that come out of the ground and they're always mad just like / super evil and whatever?

ABE: Uhhhh orcs, orcs, is / that—

MIRANDA: Yes, you look like an orc except covered in shit, that's you, right now, what the hell is going on / I swear—

ABE: Stuff Happened. And if I I I I I *had a second* to pull my head together maybe a minute to recover I could sit down and talk about this, like adults, I would love to talk about this like adults. But until . . . I'll call you in a bit, just let me be me away from you for just, like, I don't know, just like *a minute*.

MIRANDA [*telenovela*]: "My love is suffocating you, / Alejandro."

ABE: Ohmyfuckinggod / stop—

MIRANDA: "Ay Dios Mio, *it's taking you over tremendously* . . ."

ABE: That's a really bad translation / so—

MIRANDA [*dropping it*]: I know I'm the worst, OK, I am fully aware of that, I know. And you live your own life and "You do you" and I'm like *this much* of your life, OK, / I get it, I know, but Alejandro—

ABE: I.Never.Said.That.

MIRANDA: If it's a bike accident, tell me it's a bike accident. If it's some new hipster *Mad Max* look, then tell me it's some new hipster *Mad Max* look. Just please, please, tell me you're OK, I need to hear that, let me know that, please give that much to me.

ABE: Do you want me to actually be OK? Or do you just want me to say it, 'cause—

MIRANDA: . . .

ABE: I'm OK.

MIRANDA: OK?

ABE: I'm gonna be fine.

MIRANDA: OK, / OK, OK.

ABE: I'm good, I'm I'm I'm—"I'm OK."

MIRANDA AND ABE: . . .

[NUNLEY *enters*.]

NUNLEY: God y'all dramatic as fuck on a weekday.
"You OK?" "I never can tell." "But we are *FAMILY tho*." Hahaha-haha it amuses me.

MIRANDA [*as she exits*]: Well my work is done here. Nunley, sell hard and keep the meat fresh; Alejandro, I dropped off a clean shirt for you, upstairs on the register, and if there is any more use for my input, well—I'll be at the office if you need me.

NUNLEY: You don't have an office, you sit with your laptop at the laundromat—

MIRANDA: IT HAS A DOOR.

NUNLEY: EVERYTHING HAS A DOOR, DOORS DONT MAKE THINGS SPECIAL.

MIRANDA: FUCK YOU LOVE YOU BYE!

ABE AND NUNLEY: Fuck you love you bye too!

[MIRANDA *is gone*.]

[. . . *Finally,* ABE *relaxes his body, releasing a sharp yell of pain, steadying, sitting.*]

NUNLEY: . . . You look *messed the fuck up, man.*

ABE: Won't happen again.

NUNLEY: Wasn't like condemning you or anything, / hold up.

ABE: I'm late.

NUNLEY: We don't open for another fifteen, you're / fine.

ABE: Need to count the register, / need to hang—

NUNLEY: Register's counted, menu's all hung up, we're good to go.

ABE: Need to change, can I do that?

NUNLEY: —Trying to be nice here, / man—

ABE: I know what you're doing, "man."

NUNLEY: You owe me some money.

ABE: She took another sandwich, / didn't she?

NUNLEY: Put it right in her / bag.

ABE: What kind?

NUNLEY: Chicken.

ABE: That's like only halfway cooked, my god really, / really, hahahahahaha.

NUNLEY: I didn't say anything.

ABE: *Hahahahahahaa* that's / disgusting, that's, that's—

NUNLEY: She just grabbed it off the shelf all like, "Abe's got it." I was like, "Does he tho?"

ABE: Hahahaha / hahahahahha.

NUNLEY: She's running around town pretending she's some gumshoe reporter wackadoodle, girl probably thinks she's going undercover against Monsanto / or some shit; she probably liked it!

ABE: *Hahahaahahahahahahahahaha*, OK, OK, uh—yeah yeah, I got her, I got her, how much is that, like six fifteen?

NUNLEY: Look at you, all specific / and what not.

ABE: Happened before, gonna happen again, I'll put it in the drawer.

NUNLEY: All of it?

ABE: Know what, how 'bout I just put in seven and you can keep the change?

NUNLEY: Two hundred twelve.

ABE: Overnight tax hikes, / huh?

NUNLEY: Not talking about the sandwich, / man.

ABE: "Well, OK / then."

NUNLEY: You know what I'm talking about, / right?

ABE: *No clue* what you're talking about.

NUNLEY: I'm talking about the safe, man.
The safe.
. . . The safe, Abe, you / hear me?

ABE: Of course I hear you, I just have no idea what the hell you're talking about, Nunley, no clue what the fuck / you're talking about.

NUNLEY: Whoa whoa whoa, man, / whoa—

ABE: You're accusing me of stealing, that's / what's happening.

NUNLEY: I'm not accusing you of anything.

ABE: So what the hell are you doing, / then?

NUNLEY: I don't know, having a a a down to earth grown-ass discussion with my friend, damn, you are messed the fuck up.

ABE: None of your business what I did on my off time, I'm at work right now, we're not friends. So.

NUNLEY AND ABE: . . .

ABE: So you want to be a professional? Right? Wanna turn this place into something bigger, uh, uh, you're always saying that, right, "something real"—well then I don't know, maybe start treating your employees like they're working for you instead of just paid friends you boss around, and yeah, I'm late, but this place opens late, people come to eat late, and I'm sorry if me walking up like twenty minutes over is tearing apart the entire fabric of your, like, reality here, but that's just how it goes. I work hard for this place, I bend till my back breaks for this place, I'm the first one on call and the last one in here at night, every night, sorry I'm late, won't happen again, I'll pay for Miranda's sandwich, thank you for counting the register, now are we done here?

NUNLEY: There's a camera in there.

ABE: . . .

NUNLEY: Just put it in—couple months ago? After the drunk guy was sleeping out here, I thought "know what, why not just put it in," just in case, why not, you know? Didn't wanna do it. Didn't wanna like spy on you guys, never did, nothing happens here, so, left it alone, but—*something happened here* . . . Haven't looked at it yet. Just wanted to talk to you first, see what's up with you first, 'cause if anyone would know, it was, 'cause I mean you *were* the last one in here last night: Right?

ABE: What if I wasn't?

NUNLEY: Abe—you're really pushing it this morning / man.

ABE: What if I wasn't? What if I wasn't?

NUNLEY: Dude, / slow-the-fuck-down.

ABE: What if I wasn't? What if I wasn't? What if I, What if I, What If
I What? What. WHAT. What. What What, what, what, what what
what what / what what what what—

NUNLEY: (It's OK man. It's OK. It's OK.)

[ABE *falls into* NUNLEY. NUNLEY *holds him.*]

It's OK. S'OK. It's gonna be OK.

ABE AND NUNLEY: . . .

ABE: (I'm scared.)

NUNLEY: You're what?

ABE: I'm so, so scared, man, I'm—

NUNLEY: OK.

ABE: I'm so *scared.*

[ABE *pulls away, straightens up.*]

I should—

NUNLEY: You should sit right down there.
You should wait till I come back with some water.
You should breathe, man, just.
Abe?
Just fucking breathe, man.

[NUNLEY *exits.* ABE *instantly calms . . . Considers . . . Exhales.* NUNLEY *returns with water.* ABE *drinks it all in one gulp.*]

NUNLEY: This about your head?

ABE: My head and my back and my—

[ABE *pulls up his pants leg. We see a huge bruise.*]

NUNLEY: . . . Start at last night. Start at the top.

ABE: There were no witnesses.

NUNLEY: —*Witnesses.*
    . . . Where at.

ABE: Bit more west.

NUNLEY: More west?

ABE: Little bit, just a, / just a little bit—

NUNLEY: The Fuck were you doing more west.

ABE: I'm sorry—

NUNLEY: No man, nononono, I'm sorry, my bad, my shit, it's not your fault, it's not man, OK, it's not your fault.

ABE: . . . Can you say that. Just. Just like one more time.

NUNLEY: Not your fault, man. Not your fault . . . Took your wallet? Phone? Keys, all that shit, what else those fuckers get?

ABE: I didn't get—I didn't—nobody robbed me, / uh—

NUNLEY: So you got everything, / kept it all, you got it?

ABE: I have, yeah, no, I got it, got it all.

NUNLEY: So someone just beat the fuck out of you and didn't even / take anything—

ABE: Wallet and keys and phone, dead, but I / got it.

NUNLEY: Oh wow wow see that shit's even more fucked up then, those guys running around at night, the fuck they called, / you know them fuckers—

ABE: Uhhhhhh Roustabouts, / right, the with the—

NUNLEY: *Fucking Roustabouts* with the masks and shit what kind of fucking gang runs around with masks and shit the fuck is that look-de-loo goddamn Kabuki bullshit, please, *masks and shit.* This ain't Gotham City but I will sure as shit Batman a mafucker upside the head someone rolls up on my ass wearing masks and shit (where my cigarettes at) Robin Hood in a hoodie mother-fuckers goddamn diamond dogs kiss my ass (you got a light man) they try that shit, round here, on me, best believe I'll karate kick *Kill Bill* those butt-hurt Muppet babies bet that on my life *I wish a motherfucker would.*

ABE: They didn't have masks. Just one guy.

NUNLEY: Still. One guy's all it takes, no *I know that*, dude it's not even / about that—

ABE: I can take it, / like—

NUNLEY: Not even about that, happens to all of us, *when I got jumped,* 'member / that—

ABE: I remember / that.

NUNLEY: When I got jumped—in Lincoln Park, which is, I don't know man which is like going to a hot dog stand and getting an ice cream cone, just bizarre stakes, / right—

ABE: "Hahahahahahaha / hahahahahaha."

NUNLEY: Just outta the blue, boom, took two weeks' pay *like a dumbass left that shit in my wallet,* ID, license, passport, shit, remember that, *I was fucked,* / 'member that?

ABE: "Right."

NUNLEY: Least you didn't get that, 'cause damn that—I'm still getting over *that*.
White guy.
See if it was me on the other end, they'd catch my black ass in a second,
But try telling someone that you got jumped by a white dude in a Cubs hat with a backpack they be be like "Which One," you know, like—
. . . It's crazy tho, at the same time, like—physically, whatever, we got you, we got Band-Aids, we got gauze, we got all that, stacks and stacks in the back, all that, right, like, but mentally—
stays there for a little while. Kinda hard to shake. But. And I know it doesn't seem like this now, I know, but Abe:
This stuff happens more than you think. To more people than you know. You're gonna be *fine*.

ABE: . . . I think it was a hate crime.

FRIDA: Ten, nine, eight, seven, six, five, four, three, two, one.

[*Instantly we're on a*—

PARK BENCH

That afternoon.

FRIDA *stands as* MIRANDA *approaches.*]

MIRANDA: Right on time?

FRIDA: Meeting at five P.M.—

MIRANDA: Show up at four fifty and you're early, show up at four fifty-five—

FRIDA: And you're right on time, look at you. Frida Vertalo.

MIRANDA: I know who you are ohmygod / of course I know who you are!

FRIDA: Miranda—

MIRANDA: Miranda Williams, yes, thank you, uh big fan, / here, so—

FRIDA: "Look at you!"

MIRANDA: I've been reading, watching, uh, copying (!) for years / and years so—

FRIDA: You're local.

MIRANDA: I'm what?

FRIDA: Your whole life, here, / yes?

MIRANDA: Oh yeah, yeah, Chicago all the way, been here since I was born, "Chi City baby!" right!

FRIDA: Right. Which suburb?

MIRANDA: Wilmette, damn it you're good! You're / really good!

FRIDA: There you go!

MIRANDA: What gave it away?

FRIDA: Hmm? Oh, well, you just told me, so, / "voila."

MIRANDA: You're good, you're / really really good!

FRIDA: Low-hanging fruit, no secret weaponry, all-knowing intuition, no, just facts and assumption and, I don't know, moxie, that's all I got; and no shame in the suburb, either; some of the best minds running this city now aren't even originally from here.

MIRANDA: Which burb are you from?

FRIDA: Born in Old Town, I'm an original.

MIRANDA: Well, "There you go."

FRIDA: And here we are in a, in a (what is this exactly) it looks like some kind of dumping compound or a trash heap, junkyard, wasteland thing—

MIRANDA: It's a park.

FRIDA: It's *a park?*

MIRANDA: My neighborhood park / actually, so—

FRIDA: *This is a park.*

MIRANDA: This is a park, it's a, yes, this is a park.

FRIDA: Woof, *parks got weird,* amiright?

MIRANDA: Right!

FRIDA: I mean some things never change but when they do—

MIRANDA: Look what happens.

FRIDA: Back in my day we had tire swings, now there's just detached truck parts, just out, *just swinging,* woof, well, Miranda, you get ten points for creative staging.

MIRANDA: We're keeping score?

FRIDA: You're doing a great twenty-five and we've only just met, let's see if we can make it a hundred, huh?

MIRANDA: I've got a story. I mean, that's what you want, right, like on / the—

FRIDA: I list a number and an address for leads that might be of interest to the Chicago community, yes—

MIRANDA: The Chicago *Latinx community.*

FRIDA: The what now?

MIRANDA: Latinx.

FRIDA: Like the X-Men, like the mutants, what's wrong with Latino?

MIRANDA: Well, it's actually a more progressive gender-nonconforming / way of embracing like a—

FRIDA: I'm just saying Latino, I'm not an X person, / Latina, Latino, woof.

MIRANDA: OK so there's, good, OK, uhhhh . . . So, I've been following you for like, you know, a while now, and since you help people, / I—

FRIDA: Case by case basis, what's the case and what's the bias?

MIRANDA: Oh, no bias, / I—

FRIDA: Then where's the fun in that?

MIRANDA: Well this story, it isn't like, fun.

FRIDA: Come on.

MIRANDA: Like I get nothing out of this, this isn't about me.

FRIDA: So you expect me to believe that you're just going out of your way at the end of a workday to put somebody else's story out into the world when you could be using your free time to do absolutely anything else.

MIRANDA: I'm unemployed and live on a couch, *literally everything but this* is my free time.

FRIDA: Wow.

MIRANDA: This, uh—this is work.

[*Passes her an envelope.* FRIDA *opens it, flips through photographs, unemotional.*]

FRIDA: Fight?

MIRANDA: An attack.

FRIDA: Where?

MIRANDA: Alley, couple blocks away.

FRIDA: Race related?

MIRANDA: Hate Crime.

FRIDA: Where's the body?

MIRANDA: Uh . . .

FRIDA: Hate Crime means he's six feet under 'cause of one thing; Race Related means he's still alive 'cause the fight was actually about many different things.

MIRANDA: It was an attack, not a fight.

FRIDA: How do you know?

MIRANDA: He told me.

FRIDA: And *there's the bias*, see, right there, that's what stops this, right there, boyfriend or brother?

MIRANDA: I—

FRIDA: Brother, where's he hiding, out here, round the corner, where, *is he waiting behind a porta potty* or a pile of scrap metal, where is he?

MIRANDA: I'm not just stashing people so they can like pop out when I summon / them.

FRIDA: He's not coming?

MIRANDA: Alejandro's late, he's on edge, he's shook up, OK, this happened last / night.

FRIDA: If he's not here then I can't help.

MIRANDA: He's coming, I promise, / trust—

FRIDA: Online or in print? . . . Your work, is it primarily online / or in print?

MIRANDA: Oh, I, it's / actually—

FRIDA: OK, you know why I came down here, five miles from work, to talk to you, in person, as the sun sets on this swampy little junkyard, / Miranda—

MIRANDA: Well it's a park, / so—

FRIDA: No it's not, look, I've been right where you are. Not so long ago, I see it, I appreciate it, I get it, I know.
You want to help. Wanna get stories out there?
You're doing the right thing.

MIRANDA: Thank / you.

FRIDA: But you need *the work*. You need *the sources*. And then you need to doublecheck the sources and the work and get back-ups, and testimonials, and a lawyer, video, voices, facts . . .

MIRANDA: I took these pictures as soon as he got home.

FRIDA: That's why the blood is dry, nobody cares when the blood is dry.
. . . Madel Das?
Northwestern student. Couple years ago. Walking home to her dorm, two in the morning, done from doing who knows what, doesn't matter.
Some guys start screaming at her, saying she should go back home, overseas, they think she's Middle Eastern but she's South Asian, born and bred in Skokie—
Kids don't know, kids don't care, trust-fund-blue-blood-dumb kids, just a whole flock of stupid.
They beat her so hard

that when her mother went to the hospital to see her baby girl it took her a good five minutes to see if she was even looking at the right body.

Five minutes. Plus the three days it took her to get out of the coma. Then the month to return her power of speech, then getting back motor ability, strength to sit up, to process food, to walk. By the time she identified her attackers it was five months later and no matter how black the blood turned way back then the scars were too dry for anybody to even imagine what they looked like when they were still wet and red; *I am not a cruel person.*

I do not try to be cold, on the contrary, I think it's my job to help people remember what it's like to feel the heat of the moment and passion and hope, if I'm lucky enough, that's my job, "if I'm lucky."

. . . But every minute that goes by is interest lost.

You don't have every single fact; the story slips even faster.

And I wish you the best of luck. And I am sorry for this impossible pain.

. . . But if he's not willing to even show his face—

ABE: He's here.

[ABE *emerges.*]

Sorry, I . . .
Sorry I'm late, but: uh, but.
. . . I'm here.

FRIDA: . . . Dramatic reveal from behind a fucking tree, twelve bonus points.

MIRANDA: (I said four fifty-five.)

ABE: And I said sorry I'm late, I didn't know we were meeting in a construction site.

MIRANDA: This is Farrington Park, says so right on the gate.

ABE: That is not a gate, that is a fence, Farrington is the name of a construction company, / Jesus, Miranda, Jesus.

MIRANDA: Oh, fuck me.

FRIDA: Called it.

ABE: Abe Williams, nice to / meet you.

FRIDA: Frida Vertalo, great trespassing with you; so, you say Abe, she says Alejandro—

ABE: Just Abe.

FRIDA: No Alejandro, why so Anglo?

ABE: Hard to spell, hard to pronounce.

MIRANDA: For them.

ABE: Uh, I mean, sure, but, but still I'm the one / that has to deal with it with them.

FRIDA: But you're the one that has to deal with it *with them*; I get it; Abe it is.

MIRANDA: (You wanna sit down?)

ABE: (I'm fine.)

MIRANDA: (Are you / sure, I mean—)

ABE: (I'm fine, / thank you.)

FRIDA: You can still *stand*, after all that, last night, you can stand?

ABE: I mean it hurts, uh—*my brain* knows that it hurts, it's supposed to, so you know, like, I understand I'm supposed to be in pain / but . . .

FRIDA: Adrenaline.

ABE: Yeah?

FRIDA: Oh yeah, your body doesn't listen to your mind unless it has to, doesn't want to, won't do it, fine now, horrifying later.

ABE: That's great.

FRIDA: Debatable. You been to the doctor?

ABE: No, uh, my insurance / is kinda—

FRIDA: You need to see a doctor, you need a diagnosis, you need to get some pills.

ABE: Some pills . . .

FRIDA: And if you can't get a doctor to give 'em to you just ask your sister (seems like she's got some *real good connects* / amiright?)

MIRANDA: *It's just Adderall* and it's only for—

FRIDA: She's got pills, *oh yeah*, she's got pills, Abe: I like you. I feel for you.

ABE: OK.

FRIDA: I like how you come into a space, I like how you're polite.

ABE: Thank you.

FRIDA: (Was that joke about the pills too much?)

ABE: (I found it really fucking funny!)

FRIDA: *Me too.* But this is fresh for you, still, and I want you to think about not just how you're feeling right now, not just that adrenaline, that rush, I want you to think about tomorrow, and the next week, and when you look back with your kids to these twenty-four hours how you'll stand up when everything's said and done, is that clear?
I want you to think if this is worth it.

ABE: . . . What happened to me
    happens to
    a a a lot of people, but: nobody ever says anything. And I wanna
    stop that.
    I wanna help.
    . . . I wanna say something.

FRIDA: . . . This is in a bar?

ABE: At first.

FRIDA: Alone?

ABE: Does that matter?

FRIDA: Yes it does.

ABE: Alone, and out of / nowhere.

FRIDA: Why?

ABE: It was late, I wanted to just breathe, be somewhere new, without,
    just without, I don't know I mean I don't know I mean you ever
    go to a bar alone?

FRIDA: . . . "And out of nowhere."

ABE: Right, and out of nowhere, this guy starts—he starts saying
    some stuff, / uh—

FRIDA: Like what?

ABE: Like asking "what I'm doing there" stuff, asking who I know,
    what I'm drinking, when I'm finished, just like asking me too
    much stuff, so, I finish my drink, I get up, and I start to go, and I
    just hear "lemme see your papers."
    And nobody else is really there.
    Just me. The bartender. And this guy, and he's—
    he's in his fifties, maybe? Early, mid fifties, no later than that—

you could tell he—
you could tell he's been in some fights, I mean he was dressed
OK, uh, button-down, pants, slacks, maybe, dressed OK, but—
Somebody you wouldn't wanna talk back to.
So I didn't.
So I pay.
And that's when he says, "Fucking wetback. Wetback spic. Fuck-
ing dirtbag wetback spic, walk. Walk outta here. Go home, get out,
jump over the fucking fence before we make it a fucking wall.
Stay away, get out, you hear me, just go."
Over and over and over.
And I move—like I'm going to go out the front door—
I move to do that, and then I immediately double back and run
out the back door, past the bar, I just push it open and I'm moving
and I'm moving and I'm flying and just when I think I'm free
somebody comes up from the side of the alley,
pounds me, fist hits my shoulder just pounds me,
and I'm down, and he's on top of me,
and it's my face, it's my nose, it's my neck,
I push back to run I try to escape just even deflect and again
it's my face, it's my nose, it's my neck,
and I barricade my chest and push against him,
I push against him
the only thing I can do is push against him: "Stop."
. . . And I get up and I run and I run and I run and it's not until
I wake up in the morning on somebody's stoop that I realize I
blacked out.
. . . I didn't—I didn't goad him on.
I didn't—parade myself, in any way, I didn't let myself live out or
what not so he could lay me out, I, *I just went out.*
Went out for some time with myself. I just went out and—
I just went out and had a few drinks and . . .
and . . . I'm sorry, / I'm, fuck, I'm, I, I'm sorry—

MIRANDA [*trying to hold him*]: It's OK. It's OK. Shhh, shhhhhh: It's OK.
It's OK.

FRIDA [*pause*]: One or a few? . . . You said you went out for "a" drink. Had "a" drink. Paid for "a" drink. Then you said, just now, you said you went out for a few.
And maybe we've flipped the script nowadays and one means a few, but back in my day a few means at least three or four, five, a lot; but who knows I'm just terrible with math and didn't bring my calculator, so.

ABE: I said a few.

FRIDA: Just now you did but / before—

ABE: I said a few.

MIRANDA: Does it matter?

FRIDA: Every single thing you're attempting to do depends on it, yes, I'd say it matters.

MIRANDA: So if he had one drink, then he's fine, but if he had two—

FRIDA: A few.

MIRANDA: That means he's asking for it?

FRIDA: You tell me.

MIRANDA: Well, I don't think it's relevant.

FRIDA: Neither do I.

MIRANDA: OK good / so—

FRIDA: But it's not about you and it's not about me and it's not about him, it's about *them*, once again, it is always about them.

MIRANDA: Then it doesn't matter what / they—

FRIDA: Please do not finish your sentence because we all know *that it is a lie*, everything you fight and campaign and push for can only survive with their support because all that matters is what-they-think.

ABE: I had a drink.

FRIDA: *A* drink.

ABE: No more than that, *I had a drink.*

FRIDA AND ABE: . . .

FRIDA: This was completely unprovoked.

ABE: Out of the blue.

FRIDA: Which they will have trouble believing, you understand. You wouldn't believe how many stories get thrown out with the smallest fraction of deniability: "He looked at me the wrong way, and then," "She was wearing a tight dress but she flicked me off," all it takes is one other thing, one other thing, but if this was completely out of the blue, that, that—
That's something new.

MIRANDA: That's not new, that's *every-single-day.*

FRIDA: Relatively speaking, sure, I mean usually these things are premeditated by work relationships . . . neighbors, proximity; but this, what you're describing, that's 1940s stuff, that's way way back stuff, that stuff's something so old that to see it again is truly new; his name, license plate, et cetera, did you get it?

ABE: When he was screaming slurs to my back in a bar with one lightbulb or when he was beating the crap out of me in an alley?

FRIDA: Either/or is fine.

ABE: Neither, sorry, got busy.

FRIDA: It happens, you're gonna need his name.

MIRANDA: We know where it happened, you remember the bar, right, you can, we can just go back to the / bar—

FRIDA: He can't.

MIRANDA: I will.

FRIDA: You shouldn't.

MIRANDA: I am a reporter.

FRIDA: Oh honey, but are you *really, though?*

MIRANDA: . . . How many times does this happen. Ballpark.

FRIDA: I'm not good at math, I keep telling people / that . . .

MIRANDA: How many times do you get something and do nothing about it?
How Many Times.

EVERYONE: . . .

FRIDA: Three times a week.
Four in the summer.
Up and down in the winter, depends.

MIRANDA: On what.

FRIDA: If or not there's an election, it depends; *don't*—don't you do that, little girl—*nuh-nuh-nuh-nuh*, don't you look at me like that.

MIRANDA: I'm not looking at you like anything, not anymore, after that, I can't.
Not anymore.
You talk such a big game and you say this and print that but at the end of the day you can't do shit 'cause when push comes to shove—

FRIDA: *I do what I want.*

Never mistake me for some low-level hire, some idiot pawn to be
pushed, I answer to no one but the mirror—
do not mistake me I do my job I do exactly *What I Want.*
. . . I am the only—I am the only *one of my kind* in my line of
employment. I am the voice. The quo. The—
I am the foot in the door I am the only foot in the door for six-
teen years running that floor I do what I want I do what needs to
be done and that means I can fail *this* many times.

[*She makes a "zero" with her hand.*]

Know how many stories I do? How many, how many, you watch,
you're a fan, right, seventy-one, seventy-one stories, per year,
on your television in your newspaper on your little phone you
can find seventy-one instances where I shoot and when I strike
it is implicit that my insistence is above approach, one hundred
percent, everybody else? Doesn't matter, one, two, three strikes,
they get four more,
they get up they get down—but me,
with my position, within my *exotic disposition*:
if I presented every time a white person beats a brown body without a 360-degree rotating camera with Dolby surround sound
voice recording and four witnesses without one mark of red on
their ledger;
if I use my voice, and that call is not clarion, even once, that mic
goes mute, my foot is out of the door, and we don't get to scream
about anything down here, again, ever, not anymore.
. . . So do it.
Go undercover for your brother and get a statement,
from the bartender that feeds the man who beat someone and got
away with it,
his loyal customer, his alibi in full light, you go there and strap a
wire to your back and then you deal with the laws against that;

you find a security camera that shows people screaming but with
no words and find a lip reader to tell me within a sixty percentile
what was "possibly said,"
you find me some easy way to squeeze out as much truth as pos-
sible, you bring that for me to see and I
will click my finger on the screen and like your little blog that
will be seen and heard and felt by no one of any more importance
than some clicktivist with a bone to pick, now you look me in
the eye: I am trying to be your voice, so don't you *ever* tell me to
shut up.

EVERYONE: . . .

ABE: Would you like a cigarette?

FRIDA: I don't smoke.

ABE: Sorry, / I—

FRIDA: Yes, I want a cigarette, please give me a fucking cigarette, yes.

[*They smoke.*]

MIRANDA: . . . Do you meet with all of them?
    When they contact you?
    Like, you still remember the specifics of the statistics, right?

FRIDA: I never forget.

MIRANDA: So maybe, maybe his name doesn't matter, right, doesn't
    matter where the bar is, who was there; those are liabilities, they
    can fall apart.

FRIDA: Always do.

MIRANDA: Because it's never just the one story, no, this is about all of
    the stories, together, see, that's what's shocking: that's the story,
    forty of them, stripped of of name, location, only action remain-

ing, all those separate things they come together and say *something,* / right?

FRIDA: They need cohesion, you can't care about forty things: you care about one, and through that you see forty.

MIRANDA: I thought you weren't good at math.

FRIDA: We're talking about getting white people to care about race in the Midwest, this isn't math, it's fiction, I'm great with fiction; please continue / go go go—

MIRANDA: So uh, uh, hypothetically, / right—

FRIDA: "Hypothetically."

MIRANDA: Hypothetically you gotta find the one story that people care about.

FRIDA: You gotta find The Donny.

ABE: The What?

FRIDA: The Donny, come on—

MIRANDA: Nobody ever cares about any of the other Osmonds except for Donny.

FRIDA: (Thank you.)

MIRANDA: (I love it.) So you gotta find The Donny—he was singular, he was one of a kind, he was unimpeachable.

FRIDA: What's your credit score?

ABE: I—

FRIDA: *You're not unimpeachable,* you're not above reproach, now you seem great, and kind, and I mean no offense but—

MIRANDA: He's a good person.
OK?

And he might not look like it and he might not act like it, but in one look you know it he has depth and he has love and he has history and he is—
Our parents died. Almost a year ago. Car crash, both of them, he stepped up, he brought me in, he took care of me, he took care of our family, he works, and he votes, and he is a good friend, a good brother, to everybody, everybody.
He is a good, good man:
And that is enough.

FRIDA: . . . "And that's enough. The life story of a news reporter who keeps meeting people she can't help in office rooms, shitty apartments, and now, look, construction sites. *That's Enough*: coming this fall to NBC."

MIRANDA: I would totally watch that.

FRIDA: It'd run for years. Look: I can't properly express my—
Well, there you go, see, *I can't* express how angry what happened to you makes me, I don't know how.
You're not alone.
And that makes me even more angry.
. . . Find a way to channel that. Focus that? Because if you don't, it stays, and spreads, and that's the sickness. Not only do they give you physical pain, no, no, when someone does—
when someone does what they did to you it is deeper than skin; they are passing along a virus, and that's what makes you sick, that's what sticks inside, that's the stuff that can kill and if—
. . . Stay well.

[*Starts to exit.*]

ABE: He's a cop.

EVERYONE: . . .

ABE: They didn't want me there. Windows boarded up. People smoking. Inside. Still.

Not a normal bar. Cop bar.

. . . Didn't hear his name, didn't know his title, but when I pushed him into the wall to get away he fell down hard and as I was getting up, my eye caught the glint of his holster and his gun and his badge on the belt, the guy who did it, the man who put hands on me, the man who did all this, all this, this shit to me, he—he's a cop. He's—He's special, right?

. . . And I'm a waiter.

Didn't finish school. Tried, couldn't, never went back and, I don't know, I drink too much, sometimes, trying not to, better now, but I drink and I smoke, whenever I can, but I don't buy, 'cause I'm broke, did I mention that, I think it bears repeating, let me say it again just to be sure, I am poor as fuck, I am really really, really fucking poor and I'm dark-skinned, and I've been turned down from over thirty apartments,

and I've never gotten a job where I didn't know the owner, and I get flagged in every airport and they ask me about drugs, but all that doesn't happen as much anymore because I stopped going by my birth name so that's, that part's OK now,

I'm not—

I'm not unimpeachable. But I'm—

I am still here, I am still *alive—*

that's something not a lot of people can say once they've seen

a cop get dark *that's something*, I'm—I am *worth something* because I am still breathing, my life is worth something goddamn it, I am still somebody.

And that's—

I don't know, if you ask me, I think that makes me kinda sorta maybe unimpeachable. So.

FRIDA: . . . Nobody moves, nobody calls, everybody stays put, you *give me some time.*

[*She disappears.*]

ABE AND MIRANDA: . . .

ABE: She moves, like, really super fast, have you noticed, it's like I
   want her to have a cape, you know, / just like vrooooom—

MIRANDA: Don't do that.

ABE: Come on, "don't / do that," please.

MIRANDA: You should have *told me* and you know it *you know it you
   know it.*

ABE: Been a weird couple hours, / Miranda, so—

MIRANDA: This is some scary, scary shit, you should have told me.

ABE: I knew you could take it.

MIRANDA: I'm fucking terrified.

ABE: (Overreacting, / basically, but—)

MIRANDA: I'm, I'm what?

ABE: Well one day you're all "fuck the police" and now all of a sudden
   you're afraid of the cops, I mean I thought—

MIRANDA: Everyone should be afraid of the cops, they're scary as
   fuck, Jesus Christ; we need protection, if this story gets out there
   we need / solid protection.

ABE: She's gonna protect us.

MIRANDA: She'll protect herself; she is *nothing* like what I imagined,
   she's not here for us, she doesn't care—
   When this drops we need new locks on the door, no *fuck the door,*
   when this drops we need security, twenty-four/seven security,
   when this drops we need to call The Roustabouts, OK, / Alejandro, I'm serious.

ABE: Wow, a gang, A GANG, Miranda, / seriously—

MIRANDA: Well, who in the hell do you call when you can't call the cops, you need protection, we both do, Nunley too. Alejandro, the cops will do anything, anything, to protect their own so we need to do the same, OK, we need to regroup and look at our options, and you need, *Alejandro you need*, to tell me every single thing that happened last night or we could be in for some seriously insidious shit *we need to go home*—

ABE: No problem, I'll walk you down to the train, jump off in the burbs, catch a cab, all good, go.

MIRANDA: . . .

ABE: Oh you meant—oh you meant *my house, my home*, oh, OK, sorry, 'cause you said "home" I thought you meant back, back-back, Aunt Stephanie and Abuela and all that, not *my place*. My apartment. My couch. Not 'home' . . . You haven't paid rent in, in, in ever, Miranda, / ever, and I let it slide . . .

MIRANDA: What are you on, stop it, Alejandro, stop it, stop it right now, you're being so fucking stupid—

ABE: Don't. Call me stupid.

MIRANDA: You don't get to make demands, not now, not here, what the / hell were you even thinking in the—

ABE: Protected you, took you in, didn't ask for RENT, didn't ask for money, didn't ask for a dime, I carry you on my back, now it's bent and you wanna push it to break and break and break, with my money and my time and my apartment and my love for you holding you up, you're not in control of this, this is bigger than your control, I'm making sure we don't crash, this is all me now, *don't you ever,*
ever, ever call me stupid.
. . . This is bigger than me.

43

It's for . . . It's for everybody who can't. Everybody who's tried. Who's hurt. And who's fought. And *died*. It's for the way they treat us, the way they treated Nunley, the way they treated Dad, Dad told us to look down, he did, he told us to look down when cops came around, told us to look away, not anymore, OK, not anymore—we get to look up, for once, I'm gonna help us look up and I'm not the—
I'm not *smart*.
You're right. I'm not. And everybody knows it, everybody knows I'm—I've got my limits, OK I am *limited*.
But I don't think I'm here 'cause I'm smart.
Think I need to be used for something else. Something big. Bigger than me, so I need to stay, and see this out, 'cause if I don't then then my whole life—
My whole life meant nothing.
And I'm trying, OK. And it's rough, it is rough, last night was rough.

MIRANDA: Oh sure. Sure. "One Drink," that's rough, "sure."
Or was it a few? Was that it? Who can even remember, tho, right? "Sure."

ABE AND MIRANDA: . . .

ABE: Well, you know what?
That's not. Going to be part. Of the story.

MIRANDA: Alejandro, You Don't Drink.
Fuck the story.
You took an oath, you swore to me, you swore to yourself, you swore on them. You swore on our parents and that makes the earth move, Alejandro, you took an oath. And wherever they are they can feel that, breaking, they know that now so don't worry about what Frida thinks or what the news thinks or what the police think, you took on oath: and let me tell you, brother, that wrath is scarier than any law of the living.

[FRIDA *appears.*]

FRIDA: The place where you work, what time does it open?

ABE: Nine A.M.

FRIDA: I'll see you there at eight fifty-five, if you come at eight fifty-six I'll be gone. Miranda, immediately erase the call you made from your phone to me, *both* of you tell no one we were here—

MIRANDA: We're going to need some time to discuss.

FRIDA: It took you half a day to get in contact with me, how much time do you think it'll take them to find you?

ABE: You think they're looking for me?

FRIDA: I think my voice is the only protection you have.
I think this story could help the entire city and I think for once we can all do some good,
and I know you've got three seconds to say yes before I walk away and you both start running.

NUNLEY: *"Our Day will come—"*

[*Instantly, we see* NUNLEY *singing along to*

Amy Winehouse's version of "Our Day Will Come" as he sits in—

ANOTHER BAR

That night. Late. ABE *has tonic water.* NUNLEY *has a whiskey.*

They've been there for A While.]

ABE AND NUNLEY: . . .

ABE: This a happy song or a sad song?

NUNLEY: I know, right.

ABE: . . . Uh-huh

NUNLEY: Exactly that, man, exactly THAT.

ABE: . . . This place—I don't know, *uhhh / hhhhh . . .*

NUNLEY: This place is great, "uhhhh what," / what?

ABE: This place gets real hipster when the sun goes down, / doesn't it?

NUNLEY: It does a little bit / *hahahahahahaha.*

ABE: Doesn't it? I mean—
I mean if you're into that, / Nunley, you know, if you're into
that—

NUNLEY: Oh, no, psh, me, come on, come on,
I'm not into that shit, no, I'm hard-core.

ABE: Hard-core.

NUNLEY: Living life on the edge, living past life mafucker, / Past Life
What!

ABE: "Past Life What!" / Hahahahahahaha—uh-huh. Right. Right
Right. . . Bddddddddddatttt, Respect! Respect! Respect!

NUNLEY: Been on these streets since the gravel *hit the dirt,* man I'm
an original mafucking G, man, hundred-percent drop-down,
nothing doing but what it does and it do original gangsta ass
nig—[*Music changes to "You Ain't Livin till You're Lovin" by
Marvin Gaye and Tammi Terrell.*] OHmygod this is my song tho
/ this is my song right now!

ABE: Hahahahaha / hahahahahaha!

NUNLEY: Yes, yes, yes, that's what I'm talking about, / yes!

ABE: This music in here / it's—

NUNLEY: Pretty tight, right?

ABE: Varied and eclectic—

NUNLEY: Some old shit, some new shit, some middle shit you forget you even used to roll with, you like it?

ABE: I dig it.

NUNLEY: Jukebox over there, I picked like the last twenty-four songs, man. / YEAH you like it, YEAH!

ABE: Uh-huh, yeah, it sounds—sounds a lot like your car, but with, uh, more booze and e-cigarettes, so yeah, / yeah.

NUNLEY: Not like what you're used to, I know, but / still.

ABE: What I'm used to?

NUNLEY: I mean you can't smoke inside, the bartender's under eighty, no off-duty fucking law enforcement hanging around / in here, know what I mean?

ABE: "Hahahaha."

NUNLEY: See, you need to be surrounded by a big crowd of rich dark, sophisticated, *urban,* / *ethnic,* cripsity-crunchity-peanuty-buttery-chocolatey-chocolatey brown people right now.

ABE: Oh wow . . . Oh wow . . . Uh—The fuck?

NUNLEY: I have no idea what the hell I am saying I am lit the fuck up / hahahahaha!

ABE: Good to know, good to know.

NUNLEY: . . . You're safe here, man.
In here?
We got you.
And I know reporter lady scared you, alright.

Know that pressure, felt it all my life, every time I'm "out some-where I shouldn't be," anytime I talk too loud in some public place, anytime I see those bright blue lights flashing past at night I feel that pressure, man, I feel it hard all my life but you—
. . . Turn your brain off. All of it.
No one's coming for you, not here, no chance, everybody looks like you and me, you're good in here, man—
we got you.
. . . Tonic water huh. / Tonic fucking water.

ABE: Yup, good source of water and and and bubbles, / so—

NUNLEY: You want a whiskey, don't you, you-want-a-whiskey—

ABE: Not tonight, *dude DUDE.*
Not tonight.

NUNLEY: . . . I know.
Victim blaming bullshit, / believe me, I know.

ABE: What, it's not "victim blaming," OK, / it's-it's-it's not even—

NUNLEY: Can't smoke, can't drink, can't flunk out, can't talk back, can't hang out with so and so, gotta be clean, constantly, see she wants a Rosa Parks but Rosa Parks wasn't even Rosa Parks, they went through fifteen, twenty girls trying out to be *the girl* on the bus, "but she had a kid out of wedlock" "and she was too close to radicals" down-the-list till they found the one who they wanted; you're the one who she wants, look at you, man, look at you: congratulations.

ABE: . . . Like I won a prize or something.
"Congratulations," / wow, wowowow.

NUNLEY: Look man you know, OK, you know, I've been terrorized by those mafuckers my whole life / OK, alright—

ABE: Yeah well I Do Not Like Them Either / so—

NUNLEY: But they always want me a lot more than they want you.

ABE [*showing a wound on his body from the fight*]:
This is what it got me.
And on my
Chest and my neck and my ribs and my knees down to my ankles.
This is what it got me.
This is what it got me.
. . . You wish this was you?

NUNLEY: Didn't say that, / man, hold up—

ABE: You wish this was you, looking like this, feeling like this pit in
your stomach's just gonna eat you alive, looking out the window
constantly constantly just constantly scared,
And sad,
And pissed, and hating everything just everything, hating the
city you live in and used to love, hating the people sticking by
you, hating the way you never paid attention before, hating
yourself because now you're a victim, you're just a pathetic little
victim, hating yourself for being yourself, you want this to be
you?

NUNLEY: . . . Came out wrong.

ABE: K.

NUNLEY: Didn't mean it like—

ABE: Alright then.

NUNLEY: I'm sorry.

ABE: Just, just, just one more / time.

NUNLEY: I'm sorry.
I don't envy you for that.
Immense, immense shit.
. . . So no drinking / for you.

ABE: No more drinking,
That's it, it's out, don't need it, I'm good—
Have a—
Have a chance to turn over a new leaf, really mean it this time.
Makes sense, needs to happen, so yeah, YES: I'm gonna take it.

NUNLEY: . . . I mean, *I'ma* keep drinking, so / uhlılılılılı . . .

ABE: "Hahahahaha" / "so uhhhhhhhhhh" (fuck you).

NUNLEY: Just doing me, so I'm all good, don't even worry about me!
How pissed was Miranda?

ABE: Gimme a scale.

NUNLEY: Bottom level is Checkout Guy Late Night at the Jewel.
Top level is your aunt at anybody's wedding that's not her own.

ABE: I'd put it at my aunt at the wedding of the Late Night Guy from
Jewel / on top, tip-top.

NUNLEY: Daaaaaaaaaaaaamn! / Daaaaaaaaaaaaamn! Daaaaaaaaaaamn!

ABE: Just. Just. Just. Just biblical. Just—
You done?

NUNLEY: Am I— / What now, am I—

ABE: Are you done, Nunley, / are you fucking finished OK—

NUNLEY: One more, gimme one more, / man.

ABE: Take it.

NUNLEY: "DaaaaaaaaaaaaaaaaaaaaaaAaaaaaaaaaamn!"
K, I'm good.
. . . How you doing, man / like—

ABE: I'm *exhausted*.
I am . . . I am so, so tired, man. I am.
I need to, just, sorry I need to / just like—

NUNLEY: Do you man, do you.

ABE: I'm so.fucking.exhausted.

NUNLEY: . . . Wear the suit tomorrow.

ABE: It's an interview, man, like for the paper.

NUNLEY: Nah, you'll get on the TV, / watch.

ABE: Bullshit I will. Bullshit.

NUNLEY: . . . My uncle went to jail for three years 'cause he put his
    hands up in self-defense after a cop jumped him. I tell you that?
    . . . Cops were chasing some suspect, found my uncle, a goddamn
    lawyer, out of the blue jumped his ass, puts his hands up, they say
    "That's Aggressive," he says "I'm walking to my car," they give
    him prison for three years for assaulting an officer—
    He put his hands up 'cause they knock him down, man.
    Three years, man, three years.
    . . . Lawyer for twelve. One day he walked around without a suit
    they busted his ass for three years, wear-the-goddamn-suit.
    You wanna be the hero? Go ahead. Be the hero. Hella hard but
    you think you can do it—

ABE: Someone has to.

NUNLEY: Look that was my uncle, man—

ABE: Your uncle, not you, not you OK, we're talking about me.

NUNLEY: Damn right we are, 'cause if it were me—

ABE: You woulda what, what, what?

NUNLEY: . . . Take a cab.

ABE: Got my bike out here, I'm like four blocks away, five blocks, tops,
    OK, I'm / gonna bike.

NUNLEY: I'm just saying.

ABE: Look, Nunley, if I gave a fuck what you—

[*Siren in close distance. Cop lights flash by.*]

ABE AND NUNLEY: . . .

[*The cop car is gone.*]

NUNLEY [*takes out cash, hands it to* ABE]: . . . Don't care if it's four
blocks or four miles. Take a cab.

ABE: . . . I promise to never be late again.

NUNLEY: Where's this / coming from?

ABE: Uh. Mr., Mr. Brian Nunley, I promise to never be late again.
I promise to turn off the sign / every night.

NUNLEY: This about the safe?

ABE: I'm just saying, alright, I wanna get this all out before tomorrow
/ morning so—

NUNLEY: (Not talking about the god / damn safe right now.)

ABE: You think I took the money, and you think, if I took the money,
that that makes me below reproach, and if I'm below reproach,
how is anyone supposed to look at me and believe that I didn't
have a beatdown by the cops just waiting for me. And you don't
"think" that, but, but you think that, for them, 'cause it's easy to
know what they're gonna think, right?

NUNLEY: Sounds like that's what you think.

ABE: . . . Nunley, I promise to never blame other people for my shit,
'cause everybody else already has too much of their own, I promise to not ask you to lie for me, ever, ever again, I promise to try
like hell to never disappoint you again. As a person. As a friend.
As a man.

NUNLEY: What about as an employee?

ABE: Well, I can't make any promises about that, so I didn't fucking say anything.

NUNLEY: You piece of shit.

ABE: Honest piece of shit.

NUNLEY: "Fuck outta here / you piece of shit."

ABE: "See you in the morning, / Boss."

NUNLEY: Wear the suit!

ABE: Get someone to drive you home, SOMEONE NEEDS TO DRIVE YOU HOME.

NUNLEY: Don't worry about me worry about your own damn self (worry about me please) everybody's gonna drive me home baby, never a problem with that, WHAT?!

[ABE *is gone.* NUNLEY *watches him go. He finishes his drink . . . takes out a flask from his coat. Pours more. The music changes to "My Kind of Town" by Frank Sinatra, with the full introduction.*]

NUNLEY: Fuuuuuuuuuucking hipsters.—I got next! (I got next. *Damn straight* I got next.)

[NUNLEY *starts pulling out money from his wallet, crumpled up as fuck. He drinks. He counts . . .* JAMES *enters. Walks to the jukebox. Puts in a twenty. Selects a batch of songs with smooth ease. Exits . . . As he leaves, Frank Sinatra's "Chicago" starts playing.*

NUNLEY *turns around. Not having it.*

JAMES *appears with a glass of whiskey. Stands. The entire intro plays out . . . They listen.*

. . . Finally, the chorus starts: "My kind of town, Chicago is . . ."]

NUNLEY: Ohhhhh, I get it now, / I get it now.

JAMES: There it is.

NUNLEY: . . . He hated this place, didn't he?

JAMES: Fucking hated it.

NUNLEY: Blue-eyed sonofabitch, / willy-nilly piece of shit.

JAMES: That motherfucker; I'm glad he's dead.

NUNLEY AND JAMES: . . .

JAMES: Alright, you have a good night / now.

NUNLEY: Yeahyeahyeah.

JAMES: What's that?

NUNLEY: Yeah yeah, you too, man, / you too—

JAMES: OK, right, t—

[JAMES *stumbles.*]

NUNLEY: Whoa, you OK, m—

[NUNLEY *gets up to help, stumbles.*]

JAMES AND NUNLEY: . . . HAHAHAAHAHAHAHAHAHAAHAHA-
HAHAHAHAHAAHA!

JAMES: Can I—

NUNLEY: Bro you can sit here, if you can actually stand up straight
and walk, / you can sit here.

JAMES: Hahaha, Ohhhh shit shit / shit—

NUNLEY: Back?

JAMES: And my—

   And my sides and my thighs and my eyes and my gut.

NUNLEY: They got pills for all that?

JAMES [*drinking*]: Yeah, I'm taking 'em right now.

NUNLEY: Ha-ha-ha-ha that's what's up! That's what's up!

JAMES: These . . . these chairs.

NUNLEY: I know, right.

JAMES: What the hell is with these / chairs?

NUNLEY: Know why they make 'em like that?

JAMES: Why?

NUNLEY: Alright, so I don't come here often and I'm not a carpenter
   and I've never actually asked the manager but *in my professional
   opinion*—

JAMES: Yeah.

NUNLEY: Within my expertise, I'd bet that they make 'em like this so
   you don't wanna sit in 'em long, so that you drink quicker, get up
   more, drink more, sit down again / get up more, drink again—

JAMES: Oh, that's just so fucking French.

NUNLEY: Some fucked-up Frenchian shit, my normal bar, it's great,
   my normal bar they have stools.

JAMES: They should have stools, / everyone should have stools.

NUNLEY: That shouldn't even be like an additional feature.

JAMES: You shouldn't even have to tell me "they have stools," you
   should just say, "My normal bar, it's great," and I should just
   think, "Oh, it's a bar, that's great, well then they / must have
   fucking stools there," God Almighty Damn.

NUNLEY: They have fucking stools there! It's already implied! It is not a bonus reveal!

JAMES: My normal bar—

NUNLEY: Where they have stools—

JAMES: Of course they have stools.

NUNLEY AND JAMES: Goes without saying, moving on, anyway—

JAMES: My old bar doesn't have a jukebox 'cause they don't need a jukebox—
You just go up to Bartender (just walk on up), you just go up and you say, "Hey! Mikey! Play my three songs next, put it on my tab!"

NUNLEY: "Hey! Mikey!"

JAMES: No, no not like that, / no—

NUNLEY: (Is it like from the throat?)

JAMES: Just like this, "HEY, MIKEY! HEY! PLAY MY—" hahahahahahaahahaha.

NUNLEY: Hahahahahaahaha!
Oh man, if I did that here they would perform the sign of the cross, jump on all their phones, and scream for every goddamn cop on the block.

JAMES: Oh, they wouldn't call the cops.

NUNLEY: OH, they would SCREAM for the cops—

JAMES: They wouldn't scream, they'd just whisper.

[*Raises his coat.*

We see his badge on his belt.

And his gun.

NUNLEY *goes into a different mode completely.*

Trying to stay calm amid a brand-new tension.

The bar is shutting down during the rest of the scene; lights fade slowly . . .]

> . . . "Hey, Mikey!"
> Hahaha. We yell 'cause, 'cause Mikey he, he's got some weird-fuckeduphearingthingblahblahblah, hahaha, Mikey, Mikey's weird, uh—but that girl, that girl over there, I mean look at her, look at her she'd just raise one arm up, that's it, like a cab, I'm *woooooo*, right over there ya know! Hahaha, on the double, right?

NUNLEY: . . . What's wrong with your normal bar?

JAMES: Oh nothing, nothing's wrong with it, everybody loves it, uh—closed for the night.
Maintenance stuff. Just for the night.

NUNLEY: Close by?

JAMES: Not five, six blocks away

NUNLEY: What's the / name of it?

JAMES: What about you? Sorry, / sorry, I'm sorry—

NUNLEY: I said what's the—

JAMES: Here I am flapping about "ohh my old bar, my old bar, maintenance, ohh" and here you are, young buck, you know what's up, right, what's your old bar?

NUNLEY: . . . Depends on the night.

JAMES: What if it's a Tuesday?

NUNLEY: Cards on Tuesday.

JAMES: We do Sunday.

NUNLEY: Game Days?

JAMES: Depends on the game, I'm more of a—
I'm more of a sit down, have some, cool off, wind down, next time
you get up you're on your way out guy, I can't, can't do all the
tailgating, / you know.

NUNLEY: "Right."

JAMES: All the running around, face paint Indian bullshit, just can't /
do it.

NUNLEY: What?

JAMES: What? Tailgating. Can't do it. What?

NUNLEY: . . . Sorry. Long night, you know.

JAMES: Oh I hear you, look, it's that time of the year, OK, the days
get longer, sun's never up when you get out of work, takes a toll
on you, makes you heavy, makes you wound up, makes you dark,
'cause it's dark out, real dark, you know, you know, that's just
what happens here, you know what happens here.
. . . You got a happy lamp?

NUNLEY: . . . No I do not have a / happy lamp.

JAMES: Get a fucking happy lamp, look, best thing you can ever do
when it starts to get dark out there, you go to the Target no, no,
you go to the Costco, kid, fuck Target fuckit, you go to the Costco,
right, you get your cart over there and you go to the Costco /
OK, right?

NUNLEY: "I'm going to the Costco."

JAMES: Now you go around all the way down to aisle fourteen, back
of aisle fourteen you find the happy lamps, that's where they're
all just stacked up;

buy two, one for your bedroom, other one for wherever you
spend the most time, I put mine in the break room down at the
station,
get rid of the fluorescent crap who needs that / shit—

NUNLEY: "Who needs that fluorescent shit."

JAMES: Lemme tell you who needs it, nobody.
Nobody wants to be a nobody.
Go to Costco, aisle fourteen, get a happy lamp, be a somebody.
They should pay me for saying that.
Might make a good song. Real good song. They should pay me.

NUNLEY: You know who beat that guy last night?

JAMES: . . . Repeat that.

NUNLEY: Last night. By your bar. In the back.
Somebody beat a guy.

JAMES: . . . Trouble hearing you.
Come up a little closer.
Repeat that.
. . . I—

NUNLEY: Do You Know Who Beat Up the Latino Dude Outside Your
Bar Last Night.
. . . You hear that?

JAMES: . . . Heard that.

NUNLEY: Good, good.
Just making sure I'm coming through.

JAMES: —Don't know anything about that.

NUNLEY: About . . .

JAMES: Who beat up who, don't know anything, haven't heard.

NUNLEY: Yeah?

JAMES: Haven't heard, couldn't tell you, but—
    You heard something?
    So that's.
    . . . That's at least an interesting fact right there, that.

NUNLEY: . . . Guy walks into a bar.
    Late last night.
    Never been there before.
    Never had a reason to be there before, but he goes. And he comes in.
    And he sits down. And he has one drink.

JAMES: One drink?
    Who the hell has one drink?
    Ha.

NUNLEY: . . . Finishes it, gets called some names, tries to run away,
    gets chased, punched, kicked, knocked down, and attacked till he
    pushes back, runs and hides, passes out unconscious on a stoop.

JAMES: Called him names?

NUNLEY: Lotta names.

JAMES: Well, what kind of names?

NUNLEY: Beanbag. Spic. Wab. Wetback Border Nigger.

JAMES: OK.

NUNLEY: Yeah.

JAMES: OK.
    . . . Awful.
    Just . . . Just so goddamn awful, you know?
    My front door lady, at the station, name's Sofia, great kid, great
    kid, real smart, works hard, works late, she's a—
    she's a, she's a Hispanic, so. Great kid, / she's real smart.

NUNLEY: "Real smart."

JAMES: She, oh oh I said that already / didn't I—

NUNLEY: Said that already.

JAMES: Well I can't say it enough she's a great kid, she's real smart and I hate that she's got to live in a world where someone can do something like that to someone that's got her same color and then just walk away and go right on the next day without anybody doing anything to stop it.

NUNLEY AND JAMES: . . .

JAMES: Gotta top this off before they put up the last / call.

NUNLEY: Still got some left, that's Tullamore, here I got some, see—

[NUNLEY *takes out a flask, pours some into* JAMES'*s glass.*]

there you go, look at that, we're good, cheers.

[*They clink glasses. Drink.*]

NUNLEY: Better than running back to the bar, right?

JAMES: I clocked you from the second I saw you, son, I know what you're doing.

NUNLEY AND JAMES: . . .

JAMES: I couldn't do what you do.
Try to place myself in other people's shoes, yeah?
When I'm out, at work, and I get the call, and I go,
I try to place myself in the position of the person I'm supposed to go against. And it's hard.
I will admit that straight off, it is hard for me to look at someone who doesn't look like me

and put all my history into their heads and then say to myself,
"Oh OK, this led him to this. That led him to this. He led himself
to this,"—
it's hard, real hard, and it's hard 'cause it's impossible.
I wouldn't be me . . . if I was you, and vice versa, you admit that,
you know that; can't put my brain in somebody else's head but
I can try, in that moment, with everything I got
to be a good person.
. . . And that's a fight I don't always walk away from as a—Can't
always win that fight.
I see hundreds of people go by a day,
and that's only a fraction of the thousands that pass by, only
thing is, when I'm at work I'm in a uniform;
they can see me, I can't see them, see?
So it takes a . . .
Takes a certain kind of person to do what I do. I'm the one who
has to decide.
And it can never be wrong, 'cause if it is, I'm not the person who
gets to decide anymore, I'm the person who's dead.
. . . You see me
and you see everybody who ever did you wrong all at the same
time. That's tough that's real tough, son, I don't envy you that.
Nobody gets it unless they have to get it, but it's tough thinking
everybody wants to get you, 'cause if you don't, if you just see
the good in everybody, constantly, like me:
You mess up the one wrong time and you're dead.
. . . Now I knew
from the second I sat down
that you didn't really want to trust me. Then for a minute you did,
then another minute back to before, worse, 'cause you let yourself go.
And . . . Hahahahaha.
And—I want to say *do it*. Give in. Smile more. Relax.
But I can't.

So why should you.

You're pissed, you're on edge, you're scared and you don't wanna take it anymore:

Stay just like that.

Who am I to tell you any different.

. . . But you've got a nice air about you, it's real nice and it's one of a kind.

You're funny. You're smart. You're on the right track and if the day ever came when it was you against me please know it would be about your attitude and your questioning of my authority, not the color of your skin.

Maybe that's specific only to you.

Maybe I'm completely different when it's somebody else who looks just like you. Maybe I know exactly what happened last night,

Maybe I'm covering up for a friend,

Maybe I'm the bigoted piece of shit who did it and I am sitting right in front of you with a gun on my side and the power to do whatever the fuck I want, maybe this time the fucker won't get away, maybe this time I won't stop: "maybe maybe" *all these maybe's.*

. . . Truth is:

I'm not the guy you want.

Easy for me to say, tough for you to hear, but that's the truth.

. . . Bar's called Everson.

Corner across from the currency exchange two blocks off California. Bartender'll tell you everything you wanna know about last night and—

If I were you?

I would . . . listen to the entire story before I held one up to be the only, k? But what do I know, Right?

I wasn't even there.

. . . Next time keep the knife on your belt buckle,

nobody looks good with their hands already behind their back.

[JAMES *puts down two bills.*

Exits . . .

NUNLEY *has had his hand behind his back for much of the last part of the scene.*

He finally puts both hands on the table;

he's holding a knife.

He gasps for breath, aftershock.

The jukebox skips, over and over and over again, sound building, until we hear—]

ABE: Ten, nine, eight, seven, six, five, four, three, two, one.

[*And instantly we're in the—*

ALLEY

Next morning. FRIDA *approaches.*

ABE, *in loose running clothes, holds a suit by the hanger.*

Two coffees next to him.]

    Right.on.time

FRIDA: This place.

ABE: Hard to find.

FRIDA: Weird place.

ABE: Just takes a second—

FRIDA: Creepy place.

ABE: Just takes a second to let it sink in.

FRIDA: Smells funny,
Really funny, that oil and chocolate smell, downtown smell,
Except this isn't downtown *no* there's a used-car shop next to a
fish taco joint, *weird place.* / Over here, yesyes thank you.

ABE: Coffee? There's sugar inside, / if you maybe—

FRIDA: This is fine, don't touch it, it's mine now, it's fine, it's fine, /
we-are-fine, oh this is good, this.is.good.

[*She drinks.*]

ABE: Or, you know, just drink a big pitch-black hot cup of liquid with,
just, just no soul inside of it, at all, just for you.

FRIDA AND ABE: . . .

FRIDA: That the suit?

ABE: That it is.

FRIDA: Good form.

ABE: High trade.

FRIDA: Good form, nice color great cut—

ABE: Thank you.

FRIDA: Walmart or Target?

ABE: Kohl's, actually, / "That's more like it."

FRIDA: High roller, / look at this over here "high roller."

ABE: Spared no expense, so.

FRIDA: Left over from your parents' funeral?

ABE: Wow. You're.
You're, just, just / wow.

FRIDA: I'm good, right?

ABE: That's a word, / uh, that's a word that could, OK—

FRIDA: I'm good, I'm really, really good . . . I mean, honestly I thought you'd wear something more along the lines of yesterday's all-natural homegrown urban millennial flannel fanny-pack look, but a suit's good, suit's always good. Did you know there'd be cameras coming?

ABE: Nunley knew.

FRIDA: You listened to him, you're smart.

ABE: We're, we uh—
    "We are doing this."

FRIDA: I know, right.

ABE: "We are doing / this."

FRIDA: You didn't sleep.

ABE: Couldn't.

FRIDA: See, / you see that—

ABE: "You're good."

FRIDA: Just drink some coffee, wake the hell up, it's *good coffee*, I mean it tastes like it's store-bought even though I know you just made it in the back room of a sweaty meat shop, it's good shit.

ABE: I'm scared.
    Right now.
    . . . Really fucking scared. So.

FRIDA: . . . Heard something?

ABE: Saw it.
    . . . Was

Was out with a friend, last night,
Took a cab home, got in, couldn't—
Couldn't get to bed yet, so, and I run, usually (less now), but I'm
used to, my body's used to—
Anyway, I get my stuff on, and I go out the door, and I start
running and I'm good, and when I look down the alley at the end
of the block it's pitch black and that's fine except suddenly there's
headlights, headlights coming straight at me big bright headlights
in the dark
and I want to run, But it's too late
'cause there's a car coming, coming right past me, black car black
tints but then I see the eyes, passenger side, eyes looking right at
me, *and it's gone,* in a second, in just a quick second *like this* it's
gone down the street in the dark but they saw me—
See, uh, someone . . . who was looking for me Saw me.

FRIDA: . . . Coulda been an Uber.

ABE: Wasn't an Uber.

FRIDA: You never know, they're everywhere, coulda been Uber Eats.

ABE: It wasn't fucking Uber Eats.

FRIDA: You think it was the police?

ABE: . . .

FRIDA: Cops don't come around this place.
    Trust me. Something happens down here, the place is crawling
    with cameras before the blue even shows up, they don't care.
    Soon as they shut down that school down the block, you remem-
    ber it, years ago, google it, I covered it,
    ever since that nobody cares, nobody, that's why the streetlights
    don't work, big old potholes, they shot a white kid not two blocks
    down, it couldn't even get front section, *nobody cares,*
    So take, I don't know, solace, *pride,*

find some comfort in the fact that your neighborhood's screwed, the city's gonna buy it back, and nobody cares enough about this crap to come down and try to scare some waiter who might get on TV.

ABE: They left this on my front door.

[ABE *holds up a folded piece of paper.* FRIDA *takes it . . . reads it . . . hands it back.*]

FRIDA: Could've been from anybody.

ABE: It wasn't.

FRIDA: So let's show 'em *we're not gonna take it.*
    Not anymore.
    Let's sit down, and let's talk, and let's put this on TV and show them that there's a story here, something bigger here, we're *still here* down here.
    We still matter.
    . . . Pick a hotel.
    Downtown, any one, find one and we'll get you two nights, all expenses. You want three nights, we'll get you three nights, four, Whatever you need, I will do, because I respect the hell out of you, kid, I do.

ABE: It's not about a hotel.

FRIDA: Pick any one you want, any one you want except the Hyatt, not the Hyatt, we're banned from the Hyatt.

ABE: Tell me I'm not being insane.

FRIDA: Of course you're being insane.
    Oh honey, I hope you know that this is all crazy, this is not what sane people do.
    It's what good people do.

So. If that's, I don't know, if that's appealing to you then I'd say you're on the right track.

ABE: I'm so fucking dumb.

FRIDA: Don't say that.

ABE: No, I am, everybody knows it, everybody, and they're right, they are, I am dumb, I am so, so, so fucking stupid.

FRIDA: That's what they want you to think. Us, all of us, they want us to believe that our women are weak, simple, "loose," our young men, dumb, ignorant, stupid, slow, and *you know why*, don't you, / come on, kid, you know why, come on.

ABE: I don't know, maybe, maybe they're fucking right, OK, maybe they're fucking right.

FRIDA: . . . They tell us that
Because they want to keep us down, fighting with each other,
They do that because they know there are *more of us* than there
are of them— And if we figured out that we're just as smart. Just
as capable. Just as good?
If we knew that like they know that, then we wouldn't just ask
for better, we would demand it; that scares them, see?
Anybody who calls you stupid is a goddamn idiot and you tell
'em Frida Vertalo says so.
I've got this.
All of this.
"You're gotten."

ABE: . . . . I'm "gotten."

FRIDA: I'm trying it out, it's new, / go with it oh come on just go with it.

ABE: "I'm Frida Vertalo, Don't Worry, You're Gotten." MORNING, / you're late, for once, you-are-late—

[MIRANDA *enters from the side.*]

FRIDA: There she is! Minus fifteen points for Miranda. / "Look at you."

MIRANDA: Ran down here,
why is there a camera crew outside?

ABE: Already?

FRIDA: Oh my boys are so scared of me they come everywhere forty-five minutes early like I'm Midway airport, it's great, I'm gonna go set 'em up, you, suit, you top off this coffee please and keep it black black black.

MIRANDA: "Busy."

FRIDA: Stay like that! I've got it, OK, I've got it I've got it: you're gotten.

[*She's gone.* ABE *starts getting into his shirt and tie.*]

ABE: You know, I never, ever thought I'd be earlier than you. Like it's an impossibility. Like I'm actually, actually scared, like internally, it's really bracing.

MIRANDA: I found him.

ABE: Nunley, uh, get Nunley back here, please, I'm like freaking out right now he said he'd be here / at like—

MIRANDA: Abe—
I found him.
. . . I went out last night. And I looked.

ABE: For what?

MIRANDA: Your protection; to help your case, to get all the facts, make you unimpeachable, I did the work.

ABE: Not your job.

MIRANDA: Well, I'm unemployed, so I have a lot of extra time / on my hands.

ABE: Miranda, stay low, OK, Frida said to trust her so we trust her she's got / this.

MIRANDA: She didn't even look.

ABE: She's the best reporter around here, of course she looked, what / are you even talking about?

MIRANDA: I looked, just me, on my own.
I took your walk, from here,
I traced the steps you might have taken / that night.

ABE: You don't know . . .

MIRANDA: So I took five different paths one mile each way and it took hours and hours and hours but I still found him.
He knows.

ABE: There were no witnesses.

MIRANDA: You went to a gas station.

ABE: . . .

MIRANDA: Stumbled in. Bleeding, from the head.
Asked for Band-Aids. Hydrogen peroxide. Asked for, for— Well, nevermind, I'll just look at the receipt.
. . . Water. Gum. Cigarettes. "There's a receipt."
. . . Do you remember what you told him?

ABE: Didn't tell him anything.

MIRANDA: He said you were blackout drunk.

ABE: "Blackout," / hahaha, that's, that's like, that—

MIRANDA: You said one, then you said a few, the gas station attendant said you were blackout drunk, / wasted—

ABE: Nothing happened.

MIRANDA: And falling over into everything.

ABE: "And" nobody cares, / so—

MIRANDA: He said you were in shock and terrified and reeked of whiskey, Abe, he said—

ABE: LOOK.
...That place is off limits. Nobody else knows: and nobody cares, so don't mention it to Frida, don't mention it to Nunley. Miranda, there are cameras outside waiting, so don't.say.anything.

MIRANDA: You mean don't tell the truth.

ABE: OK, everything that I told you, happened, / OK—

MIRANDA: But there's something else there and you know it.
...Someone calls you names. You shout some stuff back? They get up in your face, you do / the same back—

ABE: Not like / that.

MIRANDA: You are my brother, I know this shit. I Know It.

ABE: *Then you know that cop needed to get hit.*
...Everything that happened—happened, OK, he called me—
He treated me like a dog, like I wasn't human, like my skin and my family, like I didn't matter. All that happened,
But the only thing is that for once, for once, for the first time *I fought back.*
For the first time I exploded. For the first time.
Doesn't matter if I threw the first punch.
Doesn't matter if I was: drunk drunk blackout drunk, doesn't matter if I started it, he needed to get hit because of all the shit they do everyday, and get away with it, not now no now they're gonna start paying for it; and he was big

And he was tough and he said, "you wanna try again you fucking spic" and we were OFF, and we took it outside and he was big and he was tough and tit for tat and tat for tit but at the end of all of it I left HIM on the ground.
For once someone like me left someone like him on the ground *but they don't need to know that.*
. . . So they won't know that.
It's not supposed to be a hundred percent.
They don't do that, so why should we.
Just the symbol.
Let me be that.
For once, OK, for once: let me matter.

MIRANDA: . . . If you want to make this into a story about someone refusing to be a victim and standing up for themselves then I will do that, for you, I will write all that, I will help you win.
But if you get on that TV and lie, then nobody but nobody will help you, nothing will change, and the next time one of us has something to say it won't matter because you made a cry mean nothing, *let me help you* mean something.

[NUNLEY, *at the door.*]

MIRANDA: . . . I'm gonna talk to Frida.
Then we'll both talk to her.
Then we'll all figure this out.
'Cause I love the fuck out of you and *that's just what you fucking do,* OK?

[MIRANDA *goes inside.* NUNLEY *lights up a smoke.*]

NUNLEY: . . . Fuck you love you bye too.
So.
Before you . . . Before you do all this, "whatever all this is" . . .

ABE: Nunley, *please*, just, just please give me a, there's something / I gotta just, just—

NUNLEY: Me first, me first man, OK? Last night I—
Last night I went back here.
I opened up the back room.
I turned on the camera, rewound it to last night,
And watched the whole thing so I can finally figure out what the hell happened with my safe.

ABE: . . . Nunley—

NUNLEY: I deleted it. Whatever was on that camera—Whatever it was—eighty-sixed it, didn't need to see it, who cares.
'Cause what's about to go down here,
Is *so much more important* than whatever the fuck is on that tape.
She's gonna put this up tonight, by tomorrow it's gonna spread, tomorrow night: national, man.
Last night—
Last night I was scared, terrified, rocked as fuck,
wanted to do something drastic, wanted to just take something back, wanted to fight back, wanted to, had the chance to, almost did it—
But I was scared.
I'm always so, so scared.
I can't be a . . . I'm not a fucking hero, OK, I'm "terrified as fuck," it's not me, not in me, not now, but you, man you:
You are.
You lead, I'll follow, *we'll follow,* 'cause we're all in this shit now and they can't get away with this, how they treat us, been treating us, getting permission now to treat us even worse, not now, not anymore, never again goddamn it *enough.*
. . . You're standing up, for all of us, and trust me, man: We're right behind you.

ABE: . . .

NUNLEY: —You OK, man?

ABE: ... I need to put on *pants.*

NUNLEY: Yeah, you do tho!

ABE: Just need to ... just need to put on pants.

NUNLEY: Backroom's open, go spruce the fuck up,
    And check out the meat in there, meat is ON DISPLAY in there,
    right-right / just check out that meat!

ABE: "Right Right Right!"

FRIDA [*entering*]: Abe, inside, mic up his shirt. Five minutes!

ABE: "Five minutes."

NUNLEY: "Thank you, five!"

FRIDA: "Thank you, five"—look at / you, you're a natural.

MIRANDA: Abe, don't put that mic on! Frida, stop, you can't do this—

FRIDA: His choice.

MIRANDA: As a journalist you can't, you know that, there is more
    to this story and right now so either protect the truth or we get
    buried underneath it.

NUNLEY: Whoa.

MIRANDA: Nunley, there's stuff you haven't heard, there's stuff I'm
    just finding out, and Frida, as someone who respects your work
    and believes in what you do, you need to listen to me when I say
    there are pressing things that you do not know.

FRIDA: And I-Don't-Care.
    ... Every time someone wants to talk,
    They back out.
    The people with voices, the first-hand people, the ones we need,
    they die.

Martyrs. So. Many. Many. Martyrs. *Done.*
We've got somebody in there who wants to put it on the line, so let him put it,
and let me protect him, and let me cover the tracks and if it's not one-hundred-percent they won't find out until one hundred thousand people know and then who gives a fuck, for once, who gives a fuck, I take the shot this time it's OUT.
I don't care. They don't. We Can't.
. . . Trust me. We're covered. We're covered completely.

MIRANDA AND FRIDA: . . .

MIRANDA: Nunley—

NUNLEY: Don't tell me.
   . . . I believe him. Good enough for me.
   . . . We need this.

[*He exits to inside the store.*]

FRIDA: . . . You found his route, draw it up, give it to me.
   We'll fix this from the back, before it airs, this afternoon, we call it patchwork, you help me for two hours I'll get you producer credit, small cut, potential for growth, people kill for producer credit.

MIRANDA: Tell me he's gonna be safe.
   I need to know that whatever happens, I need to know, so tell me. Please, please tell me.
   Tell me he's going to be safe.

FRIDA AND MIRANDA: . . .

FRIDA [*exiting inside*]: . . . We're on in ten.
   Nine, eight, seven, six, five, four, three, two, one.

ABE: I run. It's like a thing I do.

AN UPSCALE BAR

[*More upscale. More downtown.*

That night. ABE *in the same suit.*

It's worn. He looks like a mess, but a fancy mess.

The most loose we've seen him.

He holds a nice tumbler of whiskey.

Soft chill music in the background.]

ABE: . . . Sometimes when I get to a new place, like if I'm in a weird
party or a new block or the train—just in general, you know, "on
the train"—
I get in, and I glance around, and the first thing I do after I get in
and glance around is look for my way out.
"Two doors over there, window without a latch, stairs, cab across
the street," every time I'm somewhere new I need to know where
I stand and it's not it's not it's nothing something I want to do.
You know,
Some people walk into a room and find the person they're gonna
go home with.
Some see what's on the shelf, what album's playing, what books,
some people, some people walk into a room and they don't even
think about anything else except for "hi, how are you, oh look,
there's a chair, nice chair, look at that chair," that's privilege,
they've got it, I don't, I, I, I walk into a room and I want to know
what's gonna happen if and when it all comes down around me.
But not this time,
This time . . . I stayed.
And I got a mic up my shirt, "mic up his shirt," and I talked to
Her and made it look like I wasn't looking right at the camera and
she asked me questions and I told her everything that was able to
be said and now now now it is OUT.

. . . They didn't name the bar. Didn't name the cop. But it's bigger than that, it's more than that, I mean you saw the story it's not about that:

I'm *the symbol.*

Which is really fucking weird and like ohmygod but I'm cool, I'm cool with it, I'm cool.

Wanted to go out—out-out, leave the neighborhood, you know, watch the news, see it with a whole bunch of people who don't look like me, people who don't think like me. You know: white people. "Hey, hi," and *now I'm out,* out-out, and it's out-out and and now I'm here, and you're pouring me drinks and you have amazing liquor and I'm not supposed to be drinking but . . .

I'm not unimpeachable: I work a dead-end job, because my friend feels sorry for me, and my sister is stupid enough to believe in me, and I love the fuck out of them but at the same time I am going nowhere and that's not their fault but when I see them I still resent every single thing about them and that makes me a bad person but today tonight I did the right thing and that means something now and we're all gonna be fine now, it's all A-OK now *I am gotten.*

I.   *I am smart.*

. . . I'm *going back.*

In like—in like an hour, I'm going back, come on, I'm not, I'm not gonna like *disappear,* hahaha, I'm not going to like fucking fake my own death like that hipster piece of shit you saw that, on the news, *he just disappeared* and came back what a fucking jagoff, I'm not like that, I'm coming back, I never left.

Just needed some time. To see—

Just needed some time to see what people thought, after, after watching that, all that, and I think—I don't know, actually. I don't know, but I know that—

[*Frank Sinatra's "My Kind of Town" starts playing.*]

I did it.

And it might not have been one hundred percent.

But that doesn't matter, not now, because it's bigger than me now and—

And I get to be a little bit of a hero.

For once, for a night even, I get to go to sleep knowing I did something good and tomorrow—Tomorrow we're in a whole new world.

"Amen."

Hahahaha, "Amen," I'll drink to that, Amen.

[ABE *drains his drink.*

JAMES *enters, crosses next to* ABE, *sits,*

signals off for a drink.

He and ABE *make direct eye contact.*

And hold it.

There is a recognition.

And by that point . . .]